The Guru Method

Section I and II

For information contact:

GSMS Education Pty Ltd
P.O Box 3848
Marsfield NSW
2122
Australia

Table of Contents

Chapter 1: **Written Communication – Section II**

In the <u>Written Communications</u> section of the GAMSAT, essay topics given are in the form of quotations by famous individuals. Here the word 'communication' is significant as you will be marked on the quality of your thought and your ability to organise and convey your ideas and feelings to the reader.

You are expected to present a well-integrated and intelligent discussion with as much fluency and flair as you can muster.

There are no "correct" opinions to the given quotations. You will be marked on how well you argue your position or present your thoughts and support them, as well as your command of English. It would not be out of place to add that you need to demonstrate a mind capable of sound diagnosis, analysis and synthesis and to show yourself as a human being capable of empathising with others. This is after all the type of qualities a doctor should possess.

The key to managing your "page fright" is to:

- Practise writing as much as you can, as writing effectively is a skill that many candidates have to develop.
- Do background reading: aim to be informed. Evaluate the themes you are most likely to encounter in GAMSAT - Section II, and read on broad themes.
- Have someone critically assess your written essays because feedback is integral to your continual improvement.

Depending upon your personality and experience, this section will either be your hardest or easiest. In either case, it is strongly recommended that you focus on this area using a systematic approach as outlined below.

Remember that in the GAMSAT, most people will take quite an ad hoc approach to Section II, giving you the opportunity to separate yourself from the typical candidature.

What are the two essay types?

Argumentative essay

An argumentative essay requires you to evaluate the validity of the quotation, take a position, explain it and use reasons to consolidate it.

Reflective essay

A reflective essay is quite personal in that it solicits the reader's empathy. It makes two promises: emotional and intellectual.

1. Emotional – read this and you will be entertained, thrilled, shocked, saddened or uplifted.

2. Intellectual – read this and you will see the world from a different viewpoint OR read this and it will confirm what you already know.

Which quotation do I choose?

You just received the examination paper. You are staring at 10 quotations, quite at a loss about which one to choose.

You need to determine whether you can write an argumentative or a reflective essay.

First, ask yourself 4 questions:

1. Do I understand this quote?
2. Do I understand AND can I define ALL the terms in this quote?
3. Do I have a good knowledge of the concepts in this quote?
4. Which of the 5 given quotes meet the above 3 criteria?

If you can answer question 4, you can now choose a quote to write an argumentative essay.

Failing this, ask yourself 3 more questions.

5. Does this quote elicit a strong personal response?
6. Can I draw from personal experiences/reflections to illustrate this quote?
7. Which of the 5 given quotes meet the above 2 criteria?

If you can answer question 7, you can now choose a quote to write a reflective essay.

Let us go through a real life example of the power of these 7 questions at work.

We have the following quote

> *"The love of money is the root of all evil"*
> Bible

1. Do I understand this quote?

This quote has a very explicit meaning, which is that extreme materialism is bad; it contains just ONE central theme and is quite clear-cut in its meaning. This can be helpful, as my essay will be very focused. I will not have to wade through the multiple issues as raised in a quote which is more complex or more implicit in its meaning.

2. Do I understand AND can I define ALL the terms in this quote?

There are three terms and possibly a fourth term in this quote that I will need to define. Understand that by "define", it means something more than "give the literal definition". In the above quote, the three terms that need definition are the words "love", "money" and "evil" and possibly the word "root", depending on where you take your essay.

Let's take the word "love" for instance. It will not do to give the dictionary definition of the word. I am looking for a definition that will enable me to write an excellent essay, which will invariably mean that I need to look for implicit and metaphorical meaning to the word.

A possible definition of "love" could mean an undying attachment to money, that suggests a person has lost their mastery over money, that instead of controlling money, it now controls him/her.

Similarly, the term "money" could mean, the ability to affect the environment of an individual, an individual's power over his world. That money, in this case, represents a man's ego and his illusion of control over the world.

See how as I am defining the terms, the essay is taking shape as we speak?

If you only define your terms in the strictest literal dictionary sense, then your essay will lack the depth and flair to be anything more than an average essay.

3. Do I have a good knowledge of the concepts in this quote?

This is the most crucial question in order to select a good quote. Do you know what you want to talk about with this quote? Now if you are very familiar with this quote, you might even be able to recall that it is part of Timothy 6:10 in the bible and the entire line is

"For the love of money is the root of all evil: which while some coveted after, they have erred from the faith, and pierced themselves through with many sorrows."

If you are very familiar with the Bible you might be able to recall both similar and dissimilar lines like: "It is harder for a camel to pass through the eye of a needle than for a rich man to get into heaven". Remember also the story of King Midas. You might compare the often-quoted biblical derivative of "The love of money is the root of all evil" with "The Midas touch".

If you are well read in philosophy you could talk about various philosophers' approach to this issue.

You could talk about the US constitution and how the three tenets are "life, liberty and the pursuit of happiness" the last of which refers to "the love of money".

You can refer to people like Bill Gates, Warren Buffet, Kerry Packer, Rupert Murdock, if you have insights into their life, that can apply to this quote. You can refer to fictional characters such as Orson Welles's treatment of Charles Foster Kane, Dicken's Scrooge and look at how society viewed these works.

There is literally no end to what you can talk about for any given quotation because it depends on how familiar you are with the issues and themes presented. This is very important because the quality of your essay will depend to a large extent on the quality of the discussion and the examples. If you do not have great knowledge of the themes and issues implicit in the quote, you will not be able to write more than an average essay.

4. Which of the 5 given quotes meet the above 3 criteria?

Now you need to figure out whether any of the 5 given quotes fits your 3 criteria. If more than one does, you are in a great position to be able to choose the best one. If none of them fits, you will have to explore the option of writing a reflective rather than an argumentative essay.

5. Does this quote elicit a strong personal response?

In order to write a good reflective essay, your words need to convey meanings vividly and passionately. This can only happen if you have a strong personal response to the quote. If the quote does not move you strongly in the affirmative and/or in the negative (you do not have to side with one or the other exclusively) then the essay you write will be a lukewarm essay containing no passion which is the death knell for a reflective essay.

6. Can I draw from personal experiences/reflections to illustrate this quote?

The most powerful reflections are personal ones; it would be very helpful if you could write about personal experiences that serve to illustrate themes in the quote. Even if the reflections are not personal ones, write about them as if they were.

7. Which of the 5 given quotes meet the above 2 criteria?

If you answered questions 5 and 6 in the affirmative then you should choose to write a reflective essay.

What if I can't write an argumentative or a reflective essay?

If you have gone through the process of asking yourself the 7 questions and you have not been able to choose either an argumentative or a reflective essay, this means that you do not have the cultural knowledge to write anything more than an average essay.

Building the foundations of your cultural knowledge and acumen is beyond the scope of this book. If you would like to do this, I would suggest you read more widely, specifically, read more of the types of passages and authors that might appear in the GAMSAT.

What do I write about?

Planning helps with the narrative sequence of your essay. It is a small but crucial step, a road map, so to speak, for your entire essay, which will help you introduce your ideas and control your structure. The first five minutes should be used to plan, the next twenty to write and the final five minutes to revise any error in thinking or mechanics.

Brainstorming

One of the best methods of planning what you are going to write is structured brainstorming. It gets all the ideas from within you and allows you to select the best ones to illustrate your point. In the GAMSAT, if you are brainstorming, you will usually be looking for these aspects to a quote:

- The political
- The social
- The ethical
- The moral
- The religious
- The economic
- The environmental
- The historical
- The scientific/technological/medical

Each is demonstrated using the following quotation

"The reformative effect of punishment is a belief that dies hard, chiefly, I think, because it is so satisfying to our sadistic impulses."

Bertrand Russell

Political

How punishment is used as a form of political power in dictatorships vs. democracy
How punishment is used as a form of political power in Western Europe vs. America
How punishment is used as a form of political power in Europe vs. Asia

Social

Integration of criminal into society
Self-esteem of the criminal
Society's view of punishment

Ethical

The sanctity of life
Maintaining high standards of ethical conduct
Every human being deserves dignity

Moral

Right vs. Wrong
Good vs. Evil
The age limit of punishment
Punishment of different sexes

Religious

'An eye for an eye' argument
'Let he who is without sin cast the first stone'
'Vengeance is mine,' sayeth the Lord
Islamic mode of punishment

Economic

Prosperity of modern civilisation. Has the changes in punishment coincided with the increase in wealth?

Environmental

Not applicable

Historical

The changes in attitude towards punishment over time
The ancient Greeks/Romans/Chinese/Egyptians
Medieval attitudes
The slave trade
The transport of convicts to Australia

Scientific/Technological/Medical

The evolution of the death penalty – from spectacle to clinical
The evolution of the prison
The impact of technology on forensics

Of course in order for you to structure your thoughts correctly, you need to brainstorm in a structured manner. I recommend two approaches to organising your brainstorming, using either a mind map or an analytical structure.

I would use a mind map if the quote is a very complex one which comprises many possible themes and areas of discussion. A mind map will allow you to compare the many possible points of discussion, and enable you to select from them.

An analytical structure is preferred if the quote is relatively straightforward.

However, having said that, you will no doubt have a preference for one over the other, but I would suggest that you try each one out and see which one you prefer.

Mind Map

For example, the quote chosen is

"The reformative effect of punishment is a belief that dies hard, chiefly, I think, because it is so satisfying to our sadistic impulses."

Bertrand Russell

A mind map could look like the following

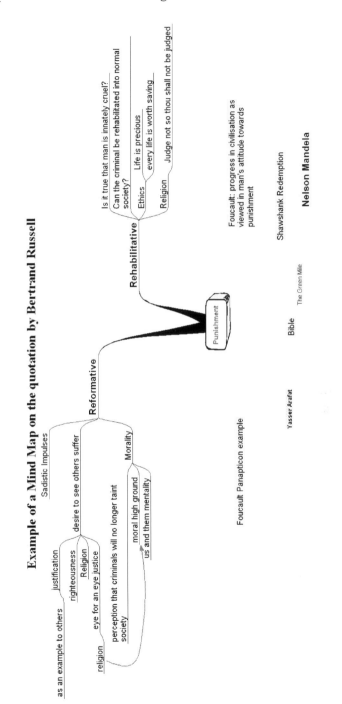

Example of a Mind Map on the quotation by Bertrand Russell

Punishment

Rehabilitative

Is it true that man is innately cruel?

Can the criminal be rehabilitated into normal society?

Ethics — Life is precious
every life is worth saving

Religion — Judge not so thou shall not be judged

Foucault: progress in civilisation as viewed in man's attitude towards punishment

Shawshank Redemption

Nelson Mandela

Bible

The Green Mile

Reformative

Sadistic Impulses

justification

desire to see others suffer

righteousness
Religion
eye for an eye justice
religion

perception that criminals will no longer taint society

Morality

moral high ground
us and them mentality

Foucault Panapticon example

Yasser Arafat

Notice the two central themes (Rehabilitative and Reformative) are branching off the quote and forming sub-branches based on possible areas of discussion, possible conclusions are included at the end of the branches. Brainstorm as many possible branches of discussion as you can within two minutes.

Notice the free floating text towards the bottom of the mind map, beneath the branches. They are examples and serve to illustrate the various points of discussion. The examples will support the conclusions that you will make in the essay. Examples will come to mind when you are drawing the branches of discussion, put these in the mind map underneath the discussion threads they support.

Analytical Structure

An analytical structure is for those who know exactly what they want to write about. If you are clear about what you want to do, use an analytical structure and refer back to it during the essay to keep you on track.

Using the same quote as the above

"The reformative effect of punishment is a belief that dies hard, chiefly, I think, because it is so satisfying to our sadistic impulses."

Bertrand Russell

Start with the conclusion in mind.

The conclusion is: Punishment has become rehabilitative rather than punitive.

Premise 1: Social argument – society has become more civilised over history
Premise 2: Moral argument – Life is precious
Premise 3: Religious argument – the emergence of secular society over fundamentalist
　　　　　　Christianity in western civilisation

Examples: examples from Foucault's writing, the Bible, the contrast between Nelson Mandela and Arafat.

Writing the argumentative essay

Writing the introduction

The introduction should consist of a general lead-in to the issue.

- (i) You might want to make an attention-getting statement.
- (ii) You can indicate that you recognise the author of the quote (if you do).
- (iii) You might give a mini-history lesson: relate some facts about the topic.
- (iv) You might start with a relevant question or two.
- (v) You can explain the key term(s).
- (vi) You can state (not debate) whether you think the claim in the quotation is a well-founded claim.
- (vii) You can then refute the claim and pose a counter-claim. Include some avenues of exploration.

So you can see that an introduction prepares the reader, gives order and direction on what is to unfold.

Now you are on your way!

Writing the body

Organise your writing in 2-3 paragraphs, expanding your ideas in the sequence of your plan. In your second paragraph, you may address counter-arguments first – that is to say, you acknowledge that your audience may have different value judgments. Then state your main premise. Explain your beliefs and justify them with your reasons. Build up your case, illustrating with examples and testimony from an authority, or from your own or a communal experience. These clarify your meanings and make distinctions of differences between viewpoints – yours and your opposition's.

In your third paragraph, introduce your second contention, explain again and illustrate. To illustrate, use facts, examples, anecdotes, comparisons and contrasts, quotations and analogies. These make abstract value terms concrete and specific.

Linking your paragraphs is crucial for a narrative flow. Group similar points together so that you can use linkages such as 'similarly', 'at the same time', or 'furthermore'. Signal a turn in the argument by using 'but', 'however', 'although' and so on.

Writing the conclusion

You should have a strong conclusion where you briefly mention the arguments in your essay and your viewpoint to come to a comprehensive ending. An ending could just be your opinion or a short quotation by someone. Be imaginative.

Framework for an excellent argumentative essay

The introduction, body, conclusion method of writing an argumentative essay has been taught in high schools since time immemorial. It is a good start, but it is not enough if you want to really take advantage of differentiating yourself from all the other candidates in the GAMSAT.

Guiding Principle

Your essay needs to be based on a guiding principle. This means that the quotation is placed into a larger context. The quote will have themes and issues that need to be explored in the argumentative essay. In order to discuss these themes and issues, we need to place the quote within a larger context, whether it is moral, philosophical, social etc…

For example:

Workers of the world unite; you have nothing to lose but your chains.

Karl Marx

This quote has themes and issues that can be discussed in terms of moral, ethical, social, political and economic dimension. We need to place this quote into one of these aspects (moral, ethical, social or economic) in order to raise the discourse above mere descriptive and explanatory examples. Anyone can agree or disagree and provide examples, but by placing the quote in a framework, we raise the standard of our essay, providing for much greater depth of discussion.

See the hierarchy of the guiding principle as applied to an imaginary essay on Communism.

Aspect: Social
Guiding principle: All workers are equal
Key Concepts: Upper classes seek to control the rest of society by controlling the modes
of production etc...

Key Concepts

The quality of your essay will depend on the depth of discussion of the key concepts that
you introduce into your essay. So during the brainstorming, really focus on getting as
many ideas out there as possible.

Key concepts are the ideas you have brainstormed that best fit into the discussion of the
quote. Remember though that the key concepts need to be related to supporting the
guiding principle.

This does not mean that the key concepts have to agree with your guiding principle, but it
does have to relate to your guiding principle.

For example:

Our guiding principle was "All workers are equal"

Key concepts:
- Upper classes seek to control the rest of society by controlling the modes of production.
- Ronald Reagan's 'trickle down economics'.
- The social effects of John Maynard Keynes's theory of comparative advantage.

See how you can relate each of these key concepts back to the guiding principle, now, if
you include a key concept like "Change in a political system can only be brought about
by revolution". This may be related to the quote but it actually detracts from the guiding
principle of "All workers are equal" because it cannot be related back to this principle.

However, if instead of choosing the social guiding principle of "All workers are equal" you
chose the political guiding principle of "Power comes from violence", then the key concept
of "Change in a political system can only be brought about by revolution" actually becomes
very relevant.

Explanations & Examples

This is the main course of the essay, if you have brainstormed well and chosen your guiding principles and key concepts well, it should practically write itself. To get into a good flow when writing this part, use tools like quotes, illustrative examples and explanations to fill out the essay.

The key here is depth; you need to be able to use explanations that illustrate the depth of your concepts. It is better to discuss in-depth fewer concepts than to discuss superficially many concepts.

The key to depth is choosing an example which you can discuss on several levels.

For example:

Concept: Change in a political system can only be brought about by revolution

Poor Example:
No communist government in the world has been elected; they have all come to power through revolution or through non-democratic means. Even with non-communist governments such as the Islamic republic of Iran, you can see that violence is the means to power. In the case where revolution was not required to change political systems, like the change to democracy from communism in Russia, you can see that democracy does not function very well there; there are lots of corruption and nepotism.

Good example:
The Allende government was democratically elected in Chile. However, in order to maintain social and economic influence in Chile, a revolution was manufactured by the US to install Pinochet. The controlling classes in any society will not allow their positions of power to be usurped by those who are powerless in that society. It is prescient that Marx predicted the failure of non-violent means of change, and also ironic that it was the US that proved his theory in this case.

You are now clear that a good example contains many different layers of meaning that is missing from a poor example.

Conclusion

Combine the concepts introduced and weld them into a central conclusion that enlightens the reader and shapes their opinions on the quote.

The conclusion should also be very straightforward if you have followed the framework around writing the argumentative essay. Instead of the usual "try to wrap up the different examples into a conclusion" trick that happens with 2 minutes to go, your guiding principle should already give you the content to write your conclusion.

For example:

Guiding principle: All workers are equal

Good conclusion: The capital of production is useless without the accompanying workforce. To insure the sustained growth of the economy, an egalitarian treatment of workers must be ensured.

Bad conclusion: Therefore, you can see that the workers need to unite in order to protect their long term future in the workforce.

Good style in argumentative essay writing

Some characteristics of good argumentative essay writing are as follows:

- Variety in sentence structure: a mixture of both long and short sentences and different sentence beginnings.
- Rich but standard vocabulary: avoidance of specialised terms or jargon, unless these are explained.
- Use of details and examples to explain and clarify abstract terms, principles and generalisations.
- Avoid unnecessary repetitions.
- Avoid short paragraphs of one or two sentences which are found in newspaper articles.
- When appropriate, use the first person 'I' or 'we' in your essay.
- Don't pad. If you cannot develop your essay with ideas, it means you have chosen a wrong quotation.

- When offering explanations, ensure that your reasons are credible.
- Finally, strive for an essay that is coherent, emphatic and unified. Coherence means that all ideas are fully explained and adequately connected by transition words such as "furthermore", "however", "in addition", "consequently" etc... The ending of one paragraph must flow on to the beginning of the next. Emphasis means the use of proper structure in your essay, with important ideas presented first. Also emphasis is also a matter of language. You may emphasise a point by using phrases such as 'it is important to realise...', 'We cannot overlook...' and the like.

Writing the reflective essay

In a reflective essay, style is important. The substance serves only to build your essay. A reflective essay is still an argument, except that it attacks a viewpoint in concrete terms using a catalogue of objects, people, events and experiences. A reflective essay relies heavily on personal experience, which in turn, provides a valuable source of knowledge and understanding.

You would normally choose a topic you can relate to, whose concepts do not need definitions.

Writing the introduction

- Focus attention
- Create interest
- Demonstrate familiarity with the quote
- Refer to the author of the quote

e.g. Take a look at the following introduction

The candlelight flickered, and a sudden gust of wind awoke the slumped figure sprawled across the oak-stained desk. His eyes glazed on the ink paused mid-sentence. "God, I wish I had a drink right now..." his eyes passed over the Courvoisier perched right above the faded copy of "Treasure Island". "When the gods wish to punish us, they answer our prayers." Oscar muttered and reached for the bottle.

See if you can find the elements outlined in the above introduction.

Writing the body

Explore the theme/subject in a variety of ways:
- Cast your mind back to recount an experience that would relate to your essay topic.

Expand:
- Explore and expand by pulling out examples from real life, from stories, films, or news events AND your own life
- Understand that some attention to specific details is crucial. However, DO NOT tell stories – they should only serve as take-off points for reflecting on the experience.

Examine:
- How did these experiences create meaning for you? What reasons had led you to your experience or your behaviour? What insights did they trigger? How has a particular incident moved you, reshaped your attitudes and values?
- Use the personal pronoun 'I' so as to relate to the reader. This provides a sense of empathy and authenticity.
- Add your emotional responses e.g. "I saw her unflinching courage – and it struck me that courage is not dependent on gender, age or one's place in life" so that there is a process of deduction.

Writing the conclusion

- Use a circular device.

  A circular device may be effective: it brings closure by referring to the beginning. On reflecting, how do you make sense of the occasion, the occurrence or experience that you described? Has it raised your self-awareness? Was there a steep learning curve? What have you learned about the human condition?
- Change to the present tense.

  Changing to the present tense brings a remembered moment back to life. For example, this sentence, 'My mother <u>places</u> flowers at the grave each anniversary' brings the reader back to the present moment and is an effective technique to conclude the essay. This shift in time is effective because it shows that having reflected on the past, you now have come back to the present moment, lesson learnt and meaning clarified.

- Use rhetorical questions.

  Rhetorical questions can be used as a means of reflection. They can be very powerful if they fit in with the style of the essay. Try to avoid using clichés like 'Is this all we have become?' 'Is this what life has become?' instead rephrase them to 'From the first moments that we crawled from our amphibian ancestors, our evolution has seen us become the dominant species on this planer, yet we are capable of such pettiness. Is this all we have become?'

- Use a clincher: 'Ah, the glamour of it all!'

e.g. Take a look at the following conclusion

All my prayers have been answered, yet instead of feeling rewarded, I feel punished. I feel doomed to a life of false expectations, doomed to a life consisting of the next prayer that needs to be answered. The doctors need to invent a new cure, the government needs to implement a new policy, the boss needs to pay me more money, the family needs to care for me more, the friends need to understand me more. Is this what I have become, the elevation of gods whom I depend upon for my salvation? Can I truly be happy, if my happiness depends on someone else answering my prayers?

See if you can discover the suggested concluding elements in the above conclusion.

We are nearly at the end….

Framework for a reflective essay

To sum up, here is a framework for a reflective essay. It consists of these elements:

ONE DAY ....**SOMETHING HAPPENED**.......................**IT ENLIGHTENED ME**
(Recall past)   (Event)   (Reflection on significance, meaning, insight, learning experience, ensuring it has a bearing to the title)

For the purpose of a 30-minute essay, you could focus on a single memorable, significant event OR you could centre your writing on a particular problem or issue and present it to the audience so that it can relate to the circumstances and make sense of them.

Stylistic elements in reflective essay writing

Use active words: I wept in frustration; I felt a surge of anger; it inflicted a pain that lasted through my youth.

Use active not passive voice: "War disrupts people" instead of "People are disrupted by war". This voice lends immediacy to the situation.

Use rhetorical devices;

- Exclamation – "What a miserable time it was!"
- Personification – "Memory came knocking at my door"
- Rhetorical question – "Are we that heartless that we can't spare even a dollar?"
- Alliteration – "Quietly and quickly she slipped away"
- Parallel constructions – "How painful it was, how succinct…."

Be eloquent, evocative, and humorous and - reflect!

GAMSAT Style Questions: Section II

ARGUMENTATIVE ESSAY

"The love of money is the root of all evil"

                      Bible

5 out of 10 essay

The word "love" in the above statement refers to an overwhelming devotion to or obsession about an object, person or hobby. The statement implies that this devotion to monetary wealth will lead to evil, unhappiness and ultimate doom. Money can lead to different paths depending on the way one views it. It can bring us joy, satisfaction and peace of mind. It can also evoke the worst human traits such as greed, corruption and selfishness. With regards to this, note that it is the "love" of money and not money itself that is the root of all evil.

Consider the gambler. As he goes to the casino, he loses money, borrows more and loses more again building up a vicious cycle which is almost impossible to break. The need and greed for more money brings about an obsessive compulsion for him. The effects trickle on towards his family and work affecting his morale and ultimately destroying the life that he once had. If destroying ones life is considered evil, then the "love" of money in this case is certainly the root of that.

On the global corporate level, society has seen the downfall of many people. Alan Bond, Christopher Skase and Nick Leeson to name some. The common lifestyle that each man possesses was that all were financially secured, they had glamorous lives and they were arguably famous. However, the obsession to "earn more" drove them to doom. They saw money as power, glamour and glory. Hence a love for money rather than people overtook their obsession and corrupted their actions. Bond and Leeson landed in prison while the late Skase went onto hiding. Here, the love of money directly led to evil.

For the ordinary family, money can make life easier. Extra educational material can be bought for a child, a surprise holiday can be treated and bills may not have to be a burden. These are some of the joys that money can bring. However, in this case, money is a requirement and is brought about by the "love" of a family and not money itself. The necessity of money here does not lead to evil but to an appreciation of what one has.

The bible says that it is the "love of money" that is the root of all evil. Money brings temptation into our lives and for those without the self-discipline for control it can certainly lead to evil and moral failure. Money should only be used as a medicine to improve one's life and spiritual self rather than be made an "obsession that leads to chasing money for its own sake. The pursuit of material for material itself is the pursuit of only living and not living well.

Critique

Introduction does not define all the terms adequately. The terms "love", "money" and "evil" must be defined and related to a larger framework. Start with a memorable opening line. This sets the tone with the marker because a strong opening line gives a strong first impression with the marker.

Cut the gambling example because it does not add to the discussion in a powerful enough way.

Delve deeper into the Alan Bond example, get rid of Skase and Leeson because it is better to focus deeper on one example rather than treat three superficially.

The fourth paragraph argues that money is necessity rather than an obsession but a better example could be used.

Strong conclusion with a powerful last sentence needed

7 out of 10 essay

Never has such a statement been so distorted. It is often said that it is "money that is the root of all evil", but the truth is revealed in the "love of money". It is often said that "love" is something that is blind, something that's an undying attachment, a sense of belonging. It is with this in mind when they penned this phrase. The undying devotion to money, this thing that is at the basis of all human dealings, it can be exchanged for every single thing on earth, money is man's ability to shape his world, money is an extension of a man's ego, money means power. With this "love of money", a man loses touch with his spirituality, and this lies at the root of all evil.

Alan Bond lived in an age where the catch cry of "greed is good" permeated all our society. He was a master of money; he became wealthy and adopted a lifestyle that was glamorous and famous. His deeds for money are even present today with the foundation of Bond University that stands as a test of his philanthropy. He became a lover of money, instead of the philanthropy of giving away money, that proved that he was master of money, instead money became the master of him, he began hoarding his money, he borrowed money to keep the money he had, he spent other peoples money when he had none left. The obsession to acquire it left him friendless; it turned the powerful charismatic icon winning the America's Cup into that frail limp figure hiding behind downcast eyes. Money became his soul nourishment, without money, his life and spirituality left him, his entire existence depended on him having money, and his deeds to acquire it and reacquire it reminds us of the lover that will do anything for his partner, he distorted that human bonding spirituality into a grotesque obsession with money, his ego was now inextricably tied with the zeros in his bank account, he debased himself with lies, fraud, he cheated friends and family. He slid slowly and surely into evil.

Is the dream to be wealthy just a planned trip into Hades? Are all rich people evil? Money can bring great happiness to a family, watch the faces of the family who are receiving a present from the Smith family at Christmas, those burdened by never ending bills, or who've never had a holiday will certainly agree that money does bring happiness. Consider Bill Gates, the richest man in the world, he gives away 2 billion dollars a year to help prevent disease in third world countries, he has left his entire fortune when he dies to charity. This man knows that he doesn't have to extend his ego by buying things to remind him of his worth, he is secured in his own place in the world. He has no need to exercise power for the sake of it; he still wears the same geeky drab as when he was a Harvard dropout with a vision for the world. He respects the power that money can bring, but his love is not an extension of his ego. His love is devotion to his wife, his cause, and his effect on the world.

A man's effect on the world needs to be measured more than how much he leaves when he dies; one competition we do not want to win is richest man in the graveyard. When a man views money as an extension of his ego, an extension of his power, then he begins a journey that culminates in the very roots of evil. Rudyard Kipling is famous for giving away all his furniture to poor families at Christmas time, when one journalist asked him why he did this, he replied very calmly, "I give them away because I own them, if I couldn't give them away, they own me."

Critique

Rephrase the first sentence clearly. Use underlining in the essay to emphasise a point. Parallelism needs work, the words "something" and "thing" should not be used in any definitions. Delete unnecessary phrases to smooth the flow of the essay.

The phrase "master of money" sounds very clichéd, it disconnects from the seriousness of the discussion. Superfluity of words reduces the essay to rambling rather than discussion.

Delete the Smith Family example, as it does not contribute to the discussion. The "Bill Gates" example needs further work, because the discussion is not passionate enough. Change the focus of the passage from one about whether rich people can have soul and spirituality to a discussion about whether society is to blame for this "love of money". This generates a more passionate discussion.

9 out of 10 essay

Never has such a statement being so distorted, it is often quoted that "money is the root of all evil", however, it is <u>the love of money</u> that is at the heart of the issue. It is often said that "love" is something that is blind, something that's an undying attachment, something that gives one a sense of belonging. Money is at the basis of all human dealings, money is man's ability to shape his world, and money is an extension of a man's ego. The undying devotion to money leads man to his pursuit of expanding the power of his ego. With this inordinate "love of money", man inevitably loses touch with his spirituality, and herein lies the root of all evil.

Alan Bond lived in an age when the catch cry of "greed is good" permeated all our society. He was a real life Gordon Gekko, he became wealthy and adopted a glamorous and hedonistic lifestyle. Bond University stands as a testament to his philanthropy. Yet in this gesture, one may question his motives, one cannot but feel that the name of the university became an expansion of his ego. The obsession to acquire money began a vicious cycle for him. It turned the powerful charismatic icon winning the America's Cup into that frail limp figure hiding behind downcast eyes. Money became his sole nourishment, without money, his life and soul left him. His entire existence depended on him having money. His obsessive attempts to acquire money reduced that unconditional love that should only be reserved for the deepest human and spiritual bonding, and is now debased into the endless acquisition of money. His bondage to the money monster he created manifests itself in his imprisonment for fraud. Bond is not an evil man, it is his love of money that has imprisoned and isolated him from his soul and humanity. It is clear that the love of money can lead any man down the same path, and herein lies the evil.

Delving further into this, is Alan Bond entirely to blame? He lives in a society that encourages people to acquire things. Consider the humble shoe, those who can display a new shoe for each day of the week are fashion experts, those who can go a month without wearing the same shoes are admired for their sexcess. It is this excess that lies at the heart of "the love of money", the acquisition of more than we can possibly use. When acquiring things become an extension of the ego, a demonstration of one's wealth and power, this is the manifestation of "the love of money". Why else would the Sultan of Brunei have a stable of 1500 luxury cars? On the other hand, consider Bill Gates, the richest man in the world, who gives away 2 billion dollars a year to help prevent disease in Third World countries. Was it "the love of money" that prompted him to bequeath his entire fortune to charity? He does not make money a part of his ego, he does not display his wealth and power in the form of acquisition excess. He still wears the same unfashionable late 70s polo shirts as when he was a Harvard dropout. He is acutely aware of the power that his money gives him, yet he is not seduced by it. His love is reserved for his devotion to his wife, his cause, and his imprint on humanity. He is empowered by his wealth rather than trapped by it, he has stared at the fork in the road and has chosen the road less travelled, and herein it made all the difference, to an entire continent of people in Africa dying from preventable diseases.

A man's effect on the world needs to be measured more than how much he leaves when he dies; one competition we do not want to win is richest man in the graveyard. When a man views money as an extension of his ego, an extension of his power, then he begins a journey that culminates in the very roots of evil. Rudyard Kipling is famous for giving away all his furniture to poor families at Christmas time, when one journalist asked him why he did this, he replied very calmly,

"I give them away because I own them, if I couldn't give them away, they own me."

Critique

The writer has gone overboard in description. The essay needs a higher philosophical musing. Add a theoretical dimension. Description is of a third level of importance in an argumentative essay. You must position your essay within a framework, explain this before illustrating. For instance, you might say that the quote relates to money behaviour.

Cut some unnecessary phrases from the essay. Make sure same thoughts are not repeated.

Rearrange the introduction to flow better. A logical structure is needed. Introduce first "money", then "love" then "love of money", cut out unnecessary phrases.

10 out of 10 essay

Never has such a statement been so distorted. It is often quoted that "money is the root of all evil". It is "the love of money", however, that is at the heart of the issue. Money is at the basis of all human dealings, it shapes the world. The undying devotion to money leads man to his pursuit of expanding the power of his ego. It is often said that "love" is a blind, undying attachment. With this inordinate "love of money", man inevitably loses touch with his spirituality, and herein lies the root of all evil.

Alan Bond lived in an age when the catch cry of "greed is good" permeated all our society. He was a real life Gordon Gekko. He became wealthy and adopted a glamorous and hedonistic lifestyle. Bond University stands as a testament to his philanthropy. Yet in this gesture, one may question his motives. One cannot but feel that the name of the university became an expansion of his ego. The obsession to acquire money began a vicious cycle for him. What became of the powerful charismatic icon who won the America's Cup? He reduced that unconditional love reserved for the deepest spiritual bonding, and debased it into the endless acquisition of money. His bondage to the money monster he created manifests itself in his imprisonment for fraud. Bond is not an evil man it is his love of money that imprisoned and isolated him from his soul and humanity. It is clear that the love of money can lead any man down the same path, and herein lies the evil.

We crave to be loved and accepted. In our personal journeys, we seek attention and connection, and often use money as that tool to do so. When we feel insecure and inadequate, money is instrumental in satisfying our desire for significance. Soon, an emotion is attached to money, and that emotion is love of money. Delving further into this, we need to ask, is Alan Bond entirely to blame? Money is an impersonal means of exchange, but a love of money injects emotion that distorts one's spiritual balance. Spiritual balance is a feeling of connection. As emotions are blindly attached to money, the love of money becomes a parasite to one's spirituality. Money now becomes a replacement for spirituality. Grotesquely, one's happiness is now measured in material wealth. Why else would the Sultan of Brunei have a stable of 1500 luxury cars?

On the other hand, consider Bill Gates, the richest man in the world, who gives away two billion dollars a year to help prevent disease in Third World countries. Was it "the love of money" that prompted him to bequeath his entire fortune to charity? He does not make money a part of his ego, he does not display his wealth and power in the form of acquisition excess. He still wears the same unfashionable late 70s polo shirts as when he was a Harvard dropout. He is acutely aware of the power that his money gives him, yet he is not seduced by it. His love is reserved for his devotion to his wife, his cause, and his imprint on humanity. He is empowered by his wealth rather than trapped by it; he has stared at the fork in the road and has chosen the road less travelled, and herein it made all the difference, to an entire continent of people in Africa dying from preventable diseases.

A man's effect on the world needs to be measured more than by how much he leaves when he dies. One competition we do not want to win is "richest man in the graveyard". When a man views money as an extension of his ego, an extension of his power, then he begins a journey that culminates in the very roots of evil. Rudyard Kipling is famous for giving away all his items of furniture to poor families at Christmas time. When one journalist asked him why he did this, he calmly replied:

"I give them away because I own them; if I couldn't give them away, they own me."

REFLECTIVE ESSAY

'When the gods wish to punish us, they answer our prayers'.

Oscar Wilde

7 out of 10 essay

How foolish Oscar Wilde must have appeared, staggering down the cobbled stones of old London town, one night in the lateness just before the habitual close of the Kangaroo Arms. He in the wisdom only conveyed by a genius in inebriation muttered forth a comment so foolish, that of all ages, it is now revered as gospel truth.

Or do we smile and nod and pass by this gem, saying only Oscar Wilde.

In these times when we more than ever fancy ourselves as gods ourselves, where everyday through the angels of biotechnology and computing, through the apostles of self-improvement and western democracy, every single of our prayers are answered, delivered to us by the higher and higher expectations that we expect from our gods and saviours.

As we live longer and longer, as we are able to lose weight without exercise, eat all the foods we want without fearing of death without at least a triple bypass to save us, spend all we want without someone who will always lend us more money without nothing but a promise and a signature.

We live the life of gods, we live a life that is only worshipped by those of our father and grandfathers. Yet Oscar Wilde, if we had been alive to witness it, him with his ruddy red cheeks, would grin and with one eye open, drawl his Irish tongue 'you fool, you are being punished."

The ease, the simplicity, each one of us now have no lack of wants, we want with abandon, accustomed to the instant satisfaction that our gods have created for the instant satisfaction that our gods have created for us. No longer do we accept that we need to exercise to remain healthy, that is now the domain of biotechnology, and our guardian angels clutching Medicare cards. No longer do we accept we need to embrace our friends, immerse ourselves in their presence, treasure just the time, second after second that we spend in their company, enjoying that unconditional companionship which breeds the life long friendships that we so desire, we now want them by attending the right schools, we want them by paying to be in the right after school program, by voting for the right candidate, by emailing the right list. No longer is a will towards dedication necessary to afford us the lap of luxury, we can now enjoy those trappings, that personalised number plate, those 300 dollar Julius Marlows. We can have the trappings, we can deceive ourselves into the state which we can enjoy the success we don't have, enjoy the health which we rent, travel the circles which we paid for.

At what cost? All our prayers have been answered, yet we are doomed. Doomed to a life of unfulfilment, doomed to a life in which we always want the next prayer to be answered. Doomed to a life which always someone else needs to answer our prayers. The doctors need to invent a new cure. The government needs to implement a new policy. The boss needs to pay us more money. The family needs to understand me more. The friends need to support me more. A life in which our happiness is but the next prayer that needs to be answered.

Oscar drawls "you poor fool, the gods are punishing you" when will it stop?

Until you have no more prayers.

Critique

It is a quite a strong introduction and a creative way to put the quote in context. It conveys familiarity with Oscar Wilde's history and his personality and lifestyle. But it could be stronger by putting a fictional spin on the quote in context, create a compelling historical introduction. Create a fictional context that demonstrates knowledge of the quote which is at the same time compelling enough to draw the marker into the essay.

The next paragraph is very vague, and contains an undeveloped concept. A plan is needed. It contains too many statements which are glossed over without a view towards in depth discussion. Overuse of parallel constructions making the paragraph sounds like the writer is inebriated. Ideas are scattered and can't be tied together.

The following paragraphs contain several themes that are introduced and developed to some extent, far better to introduce fewer concepts and develop them to a depth. Depth rather than breadth is suggested as this is a thirty minute essay.

E.g. in this essay, the following concepts are introduced such as:

1. We rely on others for our health.
2. We can borrow money too easily.
3. We live lives which our forefathers envy.
4. We don't connect with our friends now.
5. We want the trappings of success without achieving success.

Choose two themes and expand them. Being a reflective essay, choose one theme that allows you to write about a personal, emotional connection to the topic, one which will enable in depth understanding of the topic.

Concepts 4 and 5 are good choices. Number 4 allows a more personal and emotional reflection, whilst 5 allows for a deeper reflection on the topic.

It is good to end with a question because all good reflections will always raise more issues that cannot be answered in the essay, so finish with a thought-provoking question that suggests where the essay would lead to.

Clever endings are gimmicky and detracts from a good essay.

8 out of 10 essay

The candlelight flickered, and a sudden gust of wind awoke the slumped figure sprawled across the oak-stained desk. His eyes glazed over the ink paused mid-sentence. "God, I wish I had a drink right now…". His eyes passed over the Courvoisier perched right above the faded copy of "Treasure Island". "When the gods wish to punish us, they answer our prayers", Oscar muttered and reached for the bottle.

We want with abandon, accustomed to the instant satisfaction that our gods have created for us. No longer do I accept the simple pleasures that come from the bonds that are forged by unconditional friendship. In my childhood, I was happy to call my friends and breathe the same air, speak the same words, laugh at the same misfortunes, play the same games, share the same fears, feel the same anxiety. I was happy giving my time, with nothing to show for it other than that knowing we all gave. I pray for more now. I live in the time of 20-minute free calls, instant messaging, email, SMS, voicemail. I can buy my way into the right schools, I can drink my way into the right places, I can network my way into the right circles. I pray for that feeling of friendship without terms, yet, I seek it with a terms and conditions attached. Who needs one best friend, when I can now have 20 best friends? I can make 20 phone calls a week to touch base, I can do 5 power lunches a week, and I can in the throes of artificial certainty hug strangers and pretend we are the closest of friends.

We can wear the same Julius Marlows as Kerry Packer, we can wear the same Dior as Nicole Kidman, we can wear the same Tag as Steve Erwin, we can even have the same wig as Ray Martin. Is success that SLK bought on a 5 year novated lease, is success that mansion in Mosman with a 95% LVR on a first home owners grant, is success that Breitling bought on a 4.99% Amex? Our prayers have been answered, we live in the great equaliser age, every single one us can feel like a success, we can buy success, and we can live success. All those familiar trappings of success, those things we used to dream about are now available; the only exchange is a promise and a signature on a piece of paper. Why are we being punished, punished to be seeking these trappings of success, punished to measure our success by being able to acquire more and more of these, punished to never understand the full joys of earning that success and feeling it part of you. Feeling that security in living a life of success that there is no need to show the excesses of it. As Nietzsche once said, the greatest demonstration of power is not to use it when one is fully justified in doing so.

All our prayers have been answered, yet instead of feeling rewarded we feel punished. Are we doomed to a life of false expectations, doomed to a life consisting of the next prayer that needs to be answered? The doctors need to invent a new cure, the government needs to implement a new policy, the boss needs to pay me more money, the family needs to care for me more, the friends need to understand me more. Is this what our society has come to, the elevation of gods who we depend upon for our salvation? Can I truly be happy, if my happiness depends on someone else answering my prayers?

Critique

Too much speculation; too much "I can…", ad infinitum in paragraph 2. Must address the two questions, "Why are we punished?" and "How are we punished?". These are the questions that must be discussed.

9 out of 10 essay

The candlelight flickered, and a sudden gust of wind awoke the slumped figure sprawled across the oak-stained desk. His eyes glazed on the ink paused mid-sentence. "God, I wish I had a drink right now...". His eyes passed over the Courvoisier perched right above the faded copy of "Treasure Island". "When the gods wish to punish us, they answer our prayers", Oscar muttered and reached for the bottle.

We want with abandon, accustomed to the instant satisfaction that our gods have created for us. No longer do I accept the simple pleasures that come from the bonds that are forged by unconditional friendship. In my childhood, I was happy to call my friends and breathe the same air, speak the same words, laugh at the same misfortunes, play the same games, share the same fears, feel the same anxiety. Giving my time, with nothing to show for it other than that knowing we all gave. I pray for more now. I live in the time of 20-minute free calls, instant messaging, email, SMS, voicemail, I can buy my way into the right schools, I can drink my way into the right places, I can network my way into the right circles. I pray for that feeling of friendship without terms, yet, I seek it with a terms and conditions attached. A dear friend of mine called to have lunch, and that instinctive spontaneous camaraderie is replaced by the cooing voice of reason, "well wouldn't it be more efficient to organise Teppan-yaki Friday so instead of devoting 1 hour to one person, average it out so that the average friendship time is 20 minutes per person and maximise the efficacy of my platonic relationships." Oh, how wretched I felt, thinking this, I wish that the ghost of friendships past would grab me and slap into a neo-Dickensian Tarentino flick. My prayer of Mr Popularity has turned into a wretched nightmare of scrooge existence. Oh how I cursed as I reached for my chicken katsu-don.

We can wear the same Julius Marlows as Kerry Packer, we can wear the same Dior as Nicole Kidman, we can wear the same Tag as Steve Erwin, we can even have the same wig as Ray Martin. Our prayers have been answered, we live in the great equaliser age, every single one us can feel like a success, we can buy success, and we can live success. Why do I feel an adrenaline rush driving the Mercedes SLK300, stealing glances around making sure that everyone is stealing glances my way, imagining the looks of envy cast my way from strangers I will never meet. My demeanour changes, I become more confident, I slinkily slide out of my car, I exude that air of confidence that only the most ostentatious nouveau-riche can manage, until my $150 per day lease runs out. Why are we being punished, punished to be seeking these trappings of success, punished to measure our success by being able to acquire more and more of these, punished to never understand the full joys of earning that success and feeling it part of you. Feeling that security in living a life of success that there is no need to show the excesses of it. As Nietzsche once said, the greatest demonstration of power is not to use it when one is fully justified in doing so.

All our prayers have been answered, yet instead of feeling rewarded we feel punished. Are we doomed to a life of false expectations, doomed to a life consisting of the next prayer that needs to be answered? The doctors need to invent a new cure, the government needs to implement a new policy, the boss needs to pay me more money, the family needs to care for me more, and the friends need to understand me more. Is this what our society has come to, the elevation of gods who we depend upon for our salvation? Can I truly be happy, if my happiness depends on someone else answering my prayers?

Critique

A change from 'we' to 'I' adds a more personal touch. Readers relate to this. Correct grammatical and punctuation errors. Some sentences need restructuring to make meaning clear.

More reflection in the second paragraph will add intensity and depth to the example.

10 out of 10 essay

The candlelight flickered, and a sudden gust of wind awoke the slumped figure sprawled across the oak-stained desk. His eyes glazed over the ink paused mid-sentence. "God, I wish I had a drink right now…". His eyes passed over the Courvoisier perched right above the faded copy of "Treasure Island". "When the gods wish to punish us, they answer our prayers", Oscar muttered and reached for the bottle.

We want with abandon, accustomed to the instant satisfaction that our gods have created for us. No longer do I accept the simple pleasures that come from the bonds that are forged by unconditional friendship. In my childhood, I was happy to call my friends and breathe the same air, speak the same words, laugh at the same misfortunes, play the same games, share the same fears, feel the same anxiety. I gave my time, with nothing to show for it other than knowing we all gave. I pray for more now. I live in the time of 20-minute free calls, instant messaging, email, SMS, voicemail. I can buy my way into the right schools. I can drink my way into the right places. I can network my way into the right circles. I pray for that feeling of friendship without terms, yet I seek it with a terms and conditions attached. A dear friend of mine called to have lunch, and that instinctive spontaneous camaraderie is replaced by the cooing voice of reason, "Well wouldn't it be more efficient to organise Teppan-yaki Friday so instead of devoting 1 hour to one person, average it out so that the average friendship time is 20 minutes per person and thus maximise the efficacy of my platonic relationships." Oh, how wretched I felt. Thinking this, I wish that the ghost of friendships past would grab me and slap into a neo-Dickensian Tarentino flick. My prayer of Mr Popularity has turned into a wretched nightmare of scrooge existence. Oh, how I cursed as I reached for my chicken katsu-don.

We can wear the same Julius Marlows as Kerry Packer, we can wear the same Dior as Nicole Kidman, we can wear the same Tag as Steve Erwin, and we can even have the same wig as Ray Martin. Our prayers have been answered. We live in the great equaliser age, every single one us can feel like a success, we can buy success, and we can live success. Why do I feel an adrenaline rush driving the Mercedes SLK300, stealing glances around, making sure that everyone is stealing glances my way, imagining the looks of envy cast my way from strangers I will never meet. My demeanour changes, I become more confident, I slinkily slide out of my car, I exude that air of confidence that only the most ostentatious nouveau-riche can manage, until my $150 per day lease runs out. I've become that which I most despised; I am now those empty shells of success which float like deadwood down the river Styx. I've wandered down the path of the one often travelled, and I regret it every single day that I am alive. Why am I being punished, punished into seeking these trappings of success, punished into never understanding the full joys of earning that success and feeling it part of me. Why do I need to showcase my success? As Nietzsche once said, the greatest demonstration of power is not to use it when one is fully justified in doing so.

All my prayers have been answered, yet instead of feeling rewarded I feel punished. I feel doomed to a life of false expectations, doomed to a life consisting of the next prayer that needs to be answered. The doctors need to invent a new cure, the government needs to implement a new policy, the boss needs to pay me more money, the family needs to care for me more, and the friends need to understand me more. Can I truly be happy, if my happiness depends on someone else answering my prayers?

Chapter 2: **Reasoning in Humanities and Social Sciences – Section I**

The <u>Reasoning in Humanities and Social Sciences</u> section of the GAMSAT consists of passages of relative complexity followed by multiple-choice questions. All multiple-choice questions consist of a stem (the question) and a set of answer options called items. The answers are usually found in the selected passages rather than from your own corpus of knowledge.

Taking into account the tight time schedule within which you will work, you will need to be aware of the range of question-types and the strategies to deal with this section effectively.

Question types

We have placed questions into 2 categories:

1. Meaning

These will include

(a) Questions on the subject matter, main idea or purpose of the writer. Here you are asked to draw conclusions from a piece of text

(b) Interpretation of word usage. For these, use contextual clues, as meaning may not be the literal meaning but has to be interpreted in the light of the context,

(c) Questions on the author's message, the issues embedded in the text, as well as interpretation of data, diagrams and graphics.

(d) Questions asking you to explain. These usually contain the phrase '......refer to..... Scan for the given phrase in the text.

2. Implication

These will include

(a) Questions on the implications of the statements the author is making. Is the author making a value judgement? You will be expected to interpret the meanings of the author and make a determination based on what you consider the author's message to be.

(b) Questions on comparisons between 2 different passages, in terms of the difference in tone, message, theme, purpose and implied message. You will need to analyse both passages and infer meanings from them.

(c) What is suggested without expressed statements? E.g, the writer may show bias, detachment, amusement and other attitudes. This can be learned from the diction, tone or exaggerations.

Note: The GAMSAT will not directly ask for your knowledge of figurative techniques. What is a simile, metaphor, hyperbole, conceded argument, value judgement, rhetoric, personification, euphemism, oxymoron, irony, etc.? It would be useful if you understood these concepts, because you will be indirectly asked to apply this knowledge in questions.

Skimming

This is a suggested method of dealing with the given texts because of time limitation. Read actively: read with your mind not just your eyes... Do synoptic reading. Begin by skimming the passage (referred to as 'text') through, from beginning to end to obtain an overall sense of the author's subject, purpose, major ideas and information. Do not get bogged down in details. After learning the topic from the title, look first for a general sentence (or sentences) which focuses on the topic and makes a statement about the topic. Make a mental note of this. Determine the author's purpose, the contention and tone of the passage.

It is critical that you learn to skim successfully. If you read very slowly, by this I mean if you read one word at a time and vocalise words in your head, I would invest in training yourself to speed read, the amount of time wasted by slow reading could be the different between success and failure in the GAMSAT.

Key words

Do not hesitate to highlight key words, phrases, sentences, names, ideas and bits of information as you skim each passage. Do not just randomly search through the passage for the correct answer to each question.

Search scientifically. Find key word (s) or ideas in the question that are going to either contain or be near the correct answer. These are typically nouns, verbs, numbers, or phrases in the question that will probably be duplicated in the passage.

Method for answering Section I questions

It is best to skim the text first, so you have a general understanding of the passage. Do not aim for a deep understanding on your first skimming. Now read the first question. Keep the question in mind. Read the 4 answers. Keep the 4 answers in mind.

Resist the urge for your brain to immediately start looking for answers. It is critical that you keep in mind the key words in the stem and items as you return to scanning the text. It will be very rare that the key words in the stem will appear exactly in the passage. Usually you will have to keep in mind the general meaning and scan for words that have the same or similar meaning.

For example, if the stem is: "What is the author's view towards his disappointment", now when you are keyword scanning, you will be hard pressed to find the word "disappointment" exactly where the answer will lie, you will need to scan for words like "adversity, despondency, discouragement, disillusionment, dissatisfaction, regret, un-fulfillment".

If you multitask very well, you might like to scan the keywords in the items and scan for them in the passage as well.

Names, numbers or dates are also clues as to where the answer is to be found.

Questions usually correspond in chronological order to the passage i.e. the answer to the first question can be found in the first paragraph. Time will be saved if you can jump to the relevant paragraph. Your memory and visual skills will serve you well here. If you need to go back and forth from the items to the paragraph, do so rapidly. Remember, time is the essence.

If you have not found the answer right away, start with a scan of each item. Decide if each is correct or not. You may think one is correct. Mark it and return to that particular part of the passage to determine that it is indeed correct. Otherwise, look for the next best answer.

Faced with questions on inference, implication, general attitudes or themes, you think you will need an overall understanding of the passage to answer the question. This is not true. Whilst you will need an overall understanding of the text to eliminate the wrong items (distracters), the correct answer will still be found in a particular phrase or sentence contained in the text.

Remember for the harder questions, look to eliminate as many choices as possible as quickly as possible.

Be aware that GAMSAT test writers deliberately put in wrong answers to fool you. These wrong answer choices are called distracters or foils.

- They contain wrong information;
- They contain information not in the paragraph;
- They contain information that is opposite to that in the question;
- They may have a slight variation in meaning.
- They deliberately serve to advantage or disadvantage another item by contrasting with it.
- They compellingly and confusingly attract in the wrong direction.

Let's move on to the questions.

GAMSAT Style Questions: Section I

Poetry Text

Question (1-4).

Next, Please

Always too eager for the future, we	1
Pick up bad habits of expectancy	
Something is always approaching; every day	
Watching from a bluff the tiny, clear,	
Sparkling armada of promises draw near.	5
How slow they are! And how much time they waste,	
Refusing to make haste!	
Yet still they leave us holding wretched stalks	
Of disappointment, for though nothing balks	
Each big approach, leaning with brass work prinked,	10
Each rope distinct.	
Flagged, and the figurehead with golden tits	
Arching our way' it never anchors; it's	
No sooner present than it turns to past.	
Right to the last,	15
We think each one will heave to and unload	
All good into our lives, all we are owed	
For waiting so devoutly and so long	
But we are wrong.	
Only one ship is seeking us, a black-	20
Sailed unfamiliar, towing at her back	
A huge and birdless silence. In her wake	
No waters breed or break.	

Philip Larkin (1922-1985)

1. Philip Larkin's poem deals with

    A. human beings' habit of putting things off till tomorrow.

    B. the breaking of promises.

    C. disappointment.

    D. our habitual focus on the promise of the future.

2. In the second stanza, the words 'Watching from a bluff...' for 'an armada of promises tell us

    A. about our bad habits of expectancy.

    B. that financial success is always possible.

    C. that our common belief that if we wait long enough everything will come our way.

    D. of our patient nature.

3. The title, 'Next, Please' reflects our impatience to move from moment to moment, and from person to person as in a supermarket queue. This impatience is reinforced in the poem by

    A. the point that the armada 'never anchors'.

    B. the use of phrases such as 'slow', 'how much time they waste' and 'refusing to make haste'.

    C. the fact that the armada 'no sooner present than it turns to past'.

    D. the tone of disgust in the line, 'For waiting so devoutly and so long'.

4. Lines 16-17 'We think each one will heave to and unload /All good into our lives' imply that

    A. human beings are of avaricious nature.

    B. our hopes will always be undercut if we wait passively for the future.

    C. we need to work for a living.

    D. hope springs eternal in the human breast.

Shakespeare Text

Question (5–10).

The following is an extract from "The Merchant of Venice"

Portia: The quality of mercy is not strain'd   192
It droppeth as the gentle rain from heaven
Upon the place beneath: it is twice blest;
It blesseth him that gives and him that takes;
'Tis mightiest in the mightiest: it becomes
The throned monarch better than his crown,   197
His sceptre shows the force of temporal power,
The attribute to awe and majesty,
Wherein doth sit the dread and fear of kings;
But mercy is above this sceptred sway;
It is enthroned in the hearts of kings.   202
It is an attribute to God himself;
And earthly power doth then show likest God's
When mercy seasons justice. Therefore, Jew,
Though justice be thy plea, consider this,
That, in the course of justice, none of us   207
Should see salvation: we do pray for mercy;
And that same prayer doth teach us all to render
The deeds of mercy. I have spoken thus much
To mitigate the justice of thy plea;
Which if thou follow, this strict court of Venice   212
Must need give sentence 'gainst the merchant there.

Shylock
My deeds upon my head! I crave the law
The penalty and forfeit of my bond.

5. In the opening line, 'The quality of mercy is not strain'd', Portia means that

     A. mercy is as plentiful as rain.

     B. each one of us is compelled to grant mercy.

     C. mercy is free.

     D. mercy is not forced from a person.

6. The analogy between 'mercy' and 'gentle rain' takes the form of a

    A. metaphor.
    B. simile hyperbole.
    C. personification.
    D. hyperbole.

7. In her plea for mercy to be tempered with justice, the speaker dramatically uses

    A. the language of the lawyer.
    B. the language of rhetoric.
    C. the language of royalty.
    D. the language of the preacher.

8. To mitigate the justice of thy plea.....' line 211 implies that the law

    A. can be bent to suit the intention.
    B. is no respecter of persons.
    C. is unjust.
    D. can be an end in itself – inhuman and inflexible.

9. Portia's appeal to Shylock is

    A. effective.
    B. infective.
    C. insufficient
    D. compassionate yet ineffective.

10. The overall point Shakespeare makes in this passage is

    A. without mercy there is no justice
    B. mercy makes man God-like
    C. that no man can take up an absolute and immitigable point of view.
    D. mercy is an awesome and majestic quality.

Cartoon Text

Question (11-12).

US Banks overexposed to mortgages

11. The cartoonist's attitude towards banks is one of:

    A. bemusement

    B. distrust

    C. disgust

    D. cynicism

12. What set of circumstances would allow the reader to best relate to the cartoon?

    A. The falling share price of banks

    B. An interest rate increase

    C. Foreclosure of his/her house

    D. Applying for a bank housing loan

How to analyse cartoons

You would need to have a good understanding of societal norms, attitudes and values as well as an understanding of how humour and satire function. Cartoons are visual satires communicated through images. The expectation is for the audience to make a connection between the world of the cartoon and the real world. There must be something to laugh at, be it a person, thing, custom, situation or speech.

The effect of a cartoon depends on two aspects: the visual and the language aspects. Examine the images which include such features as facial expressions, clothing, positioning, unusual exaggerations and distortions in the drawings. The language aspect would include value judgements. What issues are being targeted? Are they issues of ethics or morals? Does the cartoonist use sarcasm, cynicism, scepticism, plain humour or juxtaposition to achieve his aim? Remember that incongruity is also a basic characteristic on which a cartoon works.

As an example, by studying the images and language in the above cartoon, we see the 2 characters' economic and status difference as portrayed by their clothing. The banker is perceived as glib – he glosses over issues of huge importance to individuals by replying in clichés, a ready-made answer. At the same time, the person asking the question is rather naïve. The cartoon reflects a distinct cynicism and distrust of an institution (the bank) which looms large in the life of the economy and individuals.

In answering questions on cartoons, it is suggested you look at the answer choices first; they will give you clues as to what you should look for.

Modern Prose Text

Question (13-16).

Modern Disease – Simplicity

There are some words that sound cute and fluffy. Simplicity is one of them. It implies ease and comfort. Sadly, simplicity is now a disease of the modern world because it corrodes mental stringency when its power is misunderstood.

In the fast-paced complex world, our mission is to avoid complication. We can do this by insisting on solid foundations and robust systems. The lethargic presume that promoting simplicity is the same as rejecting complications. Note that there are big differences between 'complexity' and 'complication'. The former denotes *intricacy*, while the latter denotes *difficulty*.

Albert Einstein once said 'Everything should be made as simple as possible, but not simpler.' Perhaps he was frustrated by those whose short attention-span justified their inattention to perfection.

The game of chess is like the game of life. Both can be played at superficial levels whereby obligations can continue to be met without the slightest thought about subsequent moves. Each fumbling step is justified on the basis of simplicity. Meanwhile, no strategy exists.

Their way to overcome the difficulties caused by simplicity is to learn to link your decision with your action, and your actions with your outcomes. This is a difficult process because most outcomes are separated from their original decision by time and complexity.

Beware that you do not indulge in simplicity without understanding the law of complexity. Simplicity ought to be enjoyed at the end of a project, not used in its input stages. When you work, be sure to support every act of simplicity with copious amounts of mental rigour. By all means, make your job look simple, and make every process as smooth as possible. Resist the temptation to over-burden others with systems and procedures that do not add value to the results. The message here is to become an employee who can take the most complex of elements and simplify them only when the backend processes have been thought through. Never present a simplified solution that you are unable to deconstruct.

Mathematics teachers insist that each answer must include the 'working out', because teachers are just as concerned as how you arrived at the answer. Knowing how you arrived at simplicity is the trick to sustaining it. Never trade in simplicity if you cannot deconstruct and reconstruct the whole thing (whether it is an idea, a service, or a product). No one in an organisation should be authorised to break rules or policies unless they know how they were constructed, why they were implemented and what effect they have on every other rule.

13. When the writer says 'simplicity' is a word that sounds 'warm and fuzzy', he implies that

    A. the world rejects complication.
    B. it is a word that makes people too complacent.
    C. simplicity can only be the result of deconstruction.
    D. employees do not need to be stringent in their work.

14. The second paragraph beginning, 'In the fast-paced complex world....' relates to

    A. a criticism of people who refuse to adopt simple principles.
    B. praise for people who avoid difficulties.
    C. an advice to discriminate between complexities and difficulties.
    D. criticism of the lazy or indolent.

15. From the analogy of the chess game, what does the writer think is the best way to live life?

    A. From moment to moment.
    B. By careful planning
    C. By following guiding principles.
    D. By negotiating win-win situations.

16. The one sentence that summarises the author's message is:

    A. It is only simple when you know how.
    B. Simplicity is a goal to be striven for.
    C. The world needs more simplicity..
    D. Life should be lived with careful planning.

Social Sciences Text

Question (17-20).

The top ten source countries for short-term visitor arrivals to Australia for January 2004 and the percentage and numeric change compared with January 2003 are documented in the table below.

SHORT-TERM VISITOR ARRIVALS, Major Source Countries-January 2004				
	January 2004	January 2003	Numeric Change	Percentage Change
	'000	'000	'000	%
United Kingdom	62.0	63.6	-1.6	-2.5
Japan	58.8	57.4	1.4	2.5
New Zealand	53.6	47.0	6.6	14.0
United States of America	34.1	35.2	-1.1	-3.2
China	31.2	20.8	10.4	49.7
Korea	25.9	26.0	-0.1	-0.5
Singapore	15.2	15.3	—	-0.2
Hong Kong (SAR of China)	13.0	11.4	1.6	14.1
Germany	12.1	11.7	0.4	3.4
Malaysia	10.8	8.3	2.5	30.4

17. From which group of countries did Australia experience a decrease in visitor arrivals?

    A.   Korea, Singapore, Hong Kong, Germany

    B.   China, New Zealand, Japan, United Kingdom

    C.   New Zealand, Japan, Germany, Malaysia

    D.   Singapore, United States, United Kingdom, Korea

18. From which group of countries did Australia experience the most change in the number of visitors?

    A.   Malaysia, Germany, Korea,

    B.   Hong Kong, New Zealand, Malaysia

    C.   China, New Zealand, Malaysia

    D.   Singapore, China and Korea

19. Which of the following statements is the most accurate?

    A.   The largest increase in visitor numbers were from European and North American countries

    B.   The largest increase in visitor numbers were from Asian countries

    C.   Both European and Asian countries contributed to a substantial increase in visitor numbers in the month of January

    D.   None of the above

20. Which country contributed the largest decrease to arrivals?

    A.   Singapore

    B.   Korea

    C.   United States of America

    D.   United Kingdom

Philosophy Text

Question (21-26).

The following is an extract from 'The Social Contract' by French philosopher Jean-Jacques Rousseau.

The most ancient of all societies, and the only one that is natural, is   1
the family: and even so the children remain attached to the father only
so long as they need him for their preservation. As soon as this need
ceases, the natural bond is dissolved. The children, released from the
obedience they owed to the father, and the father, released from the   5
care he owed his children, return equally to independence. If they
remain united, they continue so no longer naturally, but voluntarily;
and the family itself is then maintained only by convention.

This common liberty results from the nature of man. His first law is to
provide for his own preservation, his first cares are those which he   10
owes to himself; and, as soon as he reaches years of discretion, he is
the sole judge of the proper means of preserving himself, and
consequently becomes his own master.

The family then may be called the first model of political societies: the
ruler corresponds to the father, and the people to the children; and all,   15
being born free and equal, alienate their liberty only for their own
advantage. The whole difference is that, in the family, the love of the
father for his children repays him for the care he takes of them, while,
in the State, the pleasure of commanding takes the place of the love
which the chief cannot have for the peoples under him.   20

21. Rousseau argues that a young child's connection to its father is…

    A.   necessary yet temporary.
    B.   a learned behaviour resulting from convention.
    C.   a result of love within a family.
    D.   one of the most important institutions in modern society.

22. To what does Rousseau refer by the phrase 'This common liberty' (line 9).

    A.   The freedom that every human is born with.
    B.   Politeness and manners which people should use.
    C.   The independence which a father and child both have.
    D.   The freedom of the working classes.

23. What appears to be Rousseau's reason for discussing the family?

    A.   He wishes to explain the father/child relationship.
    B.   He has radical theories about how the child needs the father for just a short time.
    C.   He believes the father is a good example of a ruler.
    D.   He proposes that the family provides a microcosm of society.

24. Which of the following phrases is closest in meaning to line 10/11 'his first cares are those which he owes to himself'?

    A.   Children are generally selfish.
    B.   A father must put himself before his children.
    C.   A man's own concerns are more important to him than others.
    D.   Selfishness is an innate natural force and operates outside of morality.

25. What does the writer mean when he uses the phrase 'years of discretion' (line 11)

    A.   The age at which a man should be prudent.
    B.   The time of a life when a child no longer needs the father for preservation.
    C.   The age at which the father is freed from the obligation of caring from a child.
    D.   The last years of a man's life when which he should use for quiet contemplation.

26. What difference between fathers and State rulers does Rousseau refer to?

    A.   The ruler has more power than the father.
    B.   The ruler may lose power but the father cannot.
    C.   The ruler holds power for longer than the father.
    D.   They are reimbursed for their care differently.

Conceptual Thinking Text

Question (27-33).

A prior arrangement of playing cards in a specific order (unknown to the audience) is referred to as a 'stack'. Various systems exist that allow performers to know where cards in a stacked deck are located by glimpsing the face of just one card- usually the card on the bottom of the deck after the deck has been cut. A cut is a cyclical operation that transfers a group of cards from the bottom to the top of the deck without changing their order.
The following questions have to do with card order and location. The symbols used are **AS**= Ace of Spades; **2H** = Two of Hearts; **JC** = Jack of clubs; and so on in a similar fashion. Cards are listed from the top of a pack towards the bottom, when the pack is face down.

The Si-Stebbins stacking method arranges the deck with the suits of the cards in the following order: **C, H, S, D, C, H, S, D, C, H...** Since the ordering of the suits is cyclical, no matter how many times the deck is cut, if a Club appears on the bottom of the deck, the card on the top of the deck will be a Heart. A deck in Si-Stebbins stack also has the cards ordered numerically so that each card is three more than the previous with $J = 11$, $Q = 12$ and $K = 13$. When the end of a sequence is reached, counting continues again with $A = 1$. One sequence from a Si-Stebbins deck is: **6C, 9H, QS, 2D.**

27. If the bottom card of a deck in Si-Stebbins is the **AS**, what is the top card and what is the card just above the bottom card?

    A.   2D, KH
    B.   JD, 4H
    C.   KD, 4H
    D.   4D, JH

28. Counting the top card as one, if the bottom card of the deck is **10C**, what card is 7th ?

    A.   5D
    B.   4D
    C.   4H
    D.   5S

29. Counting the top card as one, if the bottom card is **JD**, at what position will the **AS** be?

    A.   14
    B.   23
    C.   26
    D.   27

Another stacking method is called 'JackAss' and uses a mnemonic to order the value of the cards. The suit order is the same as in Si-Stebbins. The mnemonic is "Jack **A**ss ate (8) live (5) tree(3), **King** intends to(2) fix(6) several(7) for(4) benign(9) **Queen.**"

Using a JackAss deck, a magician allows a spectator to cut the cards and then remove five from the top of the deck. When the deck is returned, the magician secretly glimpses the top card and then endeavors to call off the five cards the spectator is concealing.

30. The magician only wants a 80% success rate. This is thought to add drama and make the mind reading seem more 'real'. If the glimpsed card was **8H**, which of the following should the magician call off?

    A.   5S, KC, JD, 10H, 3D
    B.   5S, KC, JD, 9H, AC
    C.   QS, AC, 8H, 2S, 9H
    D.   8H, JD, 4C, QS, AC

A disadvantage of using the above two stacking methods is the inability to shuffle the pre-arranged deck in a fair manner. Decks will only retain their order after simple cuts. The next two methods are an attempt to circumvent this problem.

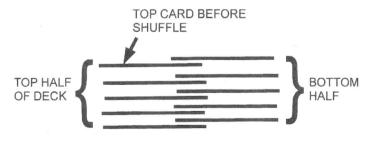

Fig 1. Faro Shuffle

Faro Shuffle: This is often described as the perfect shuffle because cards from one half of the deck are interleaved exactly evenly with the cards from the other half of the deck. The deck is split into two halves of 26 cards and shuffled together so that the original top card is second, the original second card is fourth. The 27th card becomes the top card and the 28th card becomes the third card. This is shown in Fig 1. for the new top portion of the deck, but the process is the same throughout the whole deck.

31. If a JackAss deck is faro shuffled, what two cards will appear next after a pair of black 5's?

    A.   A pair of red eights.
    B.   A pair of red threes.
    C.   A three followed by a King.
    D.   A King followed by a three.

The *Stay-stack* is an ordering of the deck that retains its character after a faro shuffle. The cards are arranged so that pairs of like color with the same value are at the same distance from the center of the deck. If the 26th card is **KS**, the 27th card will be **KC**.
The center 8 cards (in this example) could be: **8D, 5H, JC, KS, KC, JS, 5D, 8H.** Note that the pairs are not set in any order relative to other pairs, the sequence may be random. What is essential in this ordering is that each card of a pair is equidistant from the center of the deck.

32. Using the order shown in the example, what will be the third card from the top after a faro shuffle?

    A.   5H
    B.   Black King
    C.   JS
    D.   Cannot be determined.

33. A packet of 26 cards in Stay-stack order has 4C, 4S as the center pair. After how many faro shuffles will the center pair once again be the two black fours?

    A.   7
    B.   8
    C.   9
    D.   More than 9.

Solutions to GAMSAT Style Questions

1. D

This a theme question and the first few lines will usually signal what the theme is. There are two levels of meanings in poetry: the literal and the figurative. Focus on the literal first and then skim for the figurative meaning. In this question, Answer A is a possibility as the same word 'habit' appears in line 2. B is unlikely. C is likely as the word 'disappointment' was being featured in line 9, but is the poem about disappointment? D is the best answer as this reflects the theme of human beings' general habit of looking to an 'armada of promises' thinking that 'our ships will all come home' without much input on our part, and they seldom do. So though there may be identical words in the poem we need to refer to the poem to gather the general meaning and not be mislead by identical key words.

2. C

This is a question on meaning.
Sometimes the meaning of a line in a poem is not found nearby. You then need to read for global meaning: here the phrases 'wretched stalks /Of disappointment' (lines 8-9) and 'We think each one will heave to and unload / All good into our lives' (lines 12-13).

3. B

This is an application question.
You are expected to look for key words which will indicate the characteristic of human impatience and these are the words 'slow' etc. The best answer to this question is the literal one. A and C refer to the ships, which in this poem, is a metaphorical concept while D is an item on attitude.

4. B

This is a question on meaning.
This question has a similar construction as No. 2. Scan for contextual clues. The most likely two answers are B and D. Apply holistic reading for meaning. The text is

about our wishful thinking and our living in false hopes. So the choice falls on B.

5. D

Basically, this is a contextual question and in essence, is asking you the meaning of the keyword 'strain'd'. Look into how each answer fits the stem. Use the elimination technique. A describes mercy, not the meaning of the word 'strain'd'. In the distracter B, no words are synonymous to the meaning of compulsion (idea in the word 'strain'd) this leaves C and D which are opposite in meaning to B. But there is not enough evidence in C to support the idea that mercy is 'free' – you will have no time to delve into the meaning of 'free'. This leaves D as the best answer.

6. A

For the answer to this question, you will need to understand how figures of speech work. An analogy is a comparison between two objects which have similarities.

7. B

Candidates should know the word 'rhetoric'. This is the art of persuasive speech or writing. This is a good example of the implicit question. You could be easily mislead by keywords as words of a religious (God, salvation, prayer) and legal (court, sentence, justice) nature are found in the passage which is a court scene. Eliminate A and D. There is no indication that C applies.

8. D

This is an implication question.
A, C and D are the possibilities. Eliminate B as there is no suggestion of this in the speech. What is the meaning of the word 'mitigate'? And why does Portia need to ask Shylock to 'mitigate' his lawsuit? The word suggests D is the answer as without reducing the severity or rigidity of the law as befitting the circumstances, the law is an end in itself.

9. D

This is an implicit question. Do an answer scan. Ask yourself what's the impact of Portia's appeal to Shylock, the plaintiff in this court case is. Read Shylock's rejoinder.

10. B

By scanning the answers, you would eliminate C and D. Even though mercy has been linked to the words 'mightiest', 'majesty', 'awe', 'power', 'king' and 'God', is not man's nobility that Portia is appealing to. Basically she is asking him to act like a king/God who can dispense compassion.

11. D

The question asks you about the <u>cartoonist's</u> attitude. Look at the words. To the question of security, the bank manager answers in clichés – he sounds very glib and the answers are too simplistic and dismissive of greater issues related to loan securities and people's money. Eliminate A, B and C.

12. D

C can be eliminated as it would be too late if his house has been foreclosed to ask these questions. B can also be eliminated as an interest rate increase does not mean that the banking institutions are unsound. Option A may concern the customer if he is a major shareholder. The best answer is D.

13. C

Scan the key words which are in the first sentence. None of the answers correspond to the explicit meaning of 'simplicity'. Look for the underlying criticism of people's attitude to 'simplicity'. Eliminate A, B and D which are true but insufficient – they do not include a complete meaning of 'simplicity'. The answer falls on C. Look for the word 'deconstruct' and skim paragraph 5 for a holistic meaning. The question is asking you for the meaning of the text.

14. C

This is a straightforward question on the meaning of the paragraph. Use keyword scan to look for the answer. The words 'complexity' and 'difficulty' are in the last two lines of paragraph 2.

15. C

You will need to understand how an analogy works. Ask yourself what is the similarity between chess and life. Through keyword scanning you will eliminate 2 of the choices, i.e. A and D. The sentence 'Meanwhile, no strategies exists', gives you the clue – which leads you to answer choice C - guiding principles. This is a better answer than B which means a general method and not implied in the paragraph.

16. A

A question on overall theme as the word 'summarises' indicates. This means you need to read for global meaning of the passage and interpret what the writer's message is. From a brief perusal, you can eliminate 2 wrong answers – B and C. A close answer is D but this makes a more specific claim – it makes a leap into an idea that is unjustified, that is, solving problems. A is the best option as it makes a general statement of the theme.

17. D

Scan the items and find there is a listing of 4 countries per item. Here we look for countries with a decrease in arrivals. In the table there is both a percentage and numbers column. Skim for the "negative entries".

Clearly mark in you mind which countries were "negative". i.e. United Kingdom, United States, Korea and Singapore.

From now on, it is just a case of elimination.

18. C

We have a listing of countries within the four items. Skim the table to find the "high number" countries, i.e. highest change in the number of people visiting. During your skim, you should have in mind the countries that 'stand out'. Here the "high number" countries are; China, New Zealand, Hong Kong and Malaysia.

Now you should be down to choices B and C. B is tempting but note that the question asks for the "number of visitors". C is chosen by looking specifically at the number of visitors.

19. B

The greatest increase in numbers apart from New Zealand comes from China, Malaysia, Hong Kong. Some of the other items are also correct, but the most accurate answer is B.

20. D

The stem asks for the "number of visitors". Skimming the table, we look for "negative numbers" which represents the decrease in arrivals. We specifically look for the largest number in the negative direction. That country is the United Kingdom.

21. A

Rousseau states that the older child who no longer relies on the father for protection maintains a connection through convention in line 8 (B), but here we are dealing with the younger child and so lines 2 and 3, 'the children remain attached to the father only so long as they need him for their preservation' indicate that answer a best describes the connection. The love in a family (C) is cited for repaying the father for his efforts, but not for maintaining any connection between him and his child. As for (D), while Rousseau does place great importance on the family, he uses it as a metaphor for the state rather than commenting on modern society.

22. C

This answer is deduced from Rousseau's assertion that both the child and father are freed from each other when the child reaches a certain age. Answers (A) and (D) can be discounted as a result of the phrase pointing to his previous statements.

23. D

Rousseau makes correlations between the family, as the first natural society, and the State. Thus he suggests that the family is a microcosm, or miniature example of, the State. While he speaks of the father/son relationship (A) and (B), it is only to serve his wider aim of comparing it to the ruler/subject relationship. We can tell this from the fact that his conclusion moves away from his discussions of the family and summarises its parallels with the state.

24. C

Key to answering this is a recognition that the 'he' the line refers to is the hypothetical man he has been discussing, discounting answer (A). He is discussing the period of time after separation of father and son and therefore answer (B) can be discounted. Rousseau consciously avoids the moral aspect of what he discusses, discounting answer (D).

25. B

Answers (B) and (C) are both compelling, but when you recognise that the subject of this section is not the father but the son as he no longer needs the father for preservation and so 'becomes his own master' it becomes clear that the answer cannot be (C). The word 'discretion' must be read with its context firmly in mind so its other meanings, of quietude and prudence, should be discounted.

26. D

This question is an example of how important it is to read the text carefully without letting your own ideas interfere. The end of the passage sums this up, 'The whole difference is that, in the family, the love of the father for his children repays him for the care he takes of them, while, in the State, the pleasure of commanding takes the place of the love'. Rousseau does not discuss the differences in longevity or amounts of power between the father and the ruler because he is not directly comparing them but rather using one as a metaphor for the other.

27.

STEP 1 = > What do you need to determine to solve the problem?
What cards precede and follow the **AS.**

STEP 2 = > What relevant data provided in this problem are necessary to answer the question?
The card before a given card X have the value X − 3 and the card after, X + 3. The suits rotate C,H,S,D and the deck is cyclical, the 'next card' after the bottom card is the top card.

STEP 3 = > Use the relevant data to solve the question.
A = 1, adding 3 means the top card is a 4. The next suit in sequence after S is D. So the top card is the four of diamonds (4D). The card right above the AS is $1 - 3 \rightarrow$ J, and the suit is one before S, which is H. So the previous card is the JH. Answer (D).

28.

STEP 1 = > What do you need to determine to solve the problem?
The seventh card in a sequence that begins with 10C = 0.

STEP 2 = > What relevant data provided in this problem are necessary to answer the question?
The bottom card and the method of ordering the cards.

STEP 3 = > Use the relevant data to solve the question.
Increasing by 3 at each step and rotating suits in the pattern given leads to the following sequence:
10C (bottom card), KH (top card), 3S, 6D, 9C, QH, 2S, 5D – the seventh from the top is 5D, which is (A).

29.

STEP 1 = > What do you need to determine to solve the problem?
Where in the deck is the AS?

STEP 2 = > What relevant data provided in this problem are necessary to answer the question?
Given the bottom card, the top card can be determined. From that, the location of the aces can be determined. Since the suits rotate predictably, we can then find where a particular ace is.

STEP 3 = > Use the relevant data to solve the question.
If JD is on the bottom, the top card will be the AC. The next ace will be thirteen cards further down (since the ordering is cyclical in groups of 13) and the suit rotation tells us it will be AH. The next ace (thirteen more cards down) is the one we want, AS. 1 + 13 + 13 = 27. Answer (D).

30.

STEP 1 = > What do you need to determine to solve the problem?
The correct ordering for the cards removed.

STEP 2 = > What relevant data provided in this problem are necessary to answer the question?
The mnemonic tells us the order of cards is a Jackass deck and the suits rotate as before. Also, if 5 cards are removed, an 80% success rate means that we need to name 4 correctly and 1 incorrectly.

STEP 3 = > Use the relevant data to solve the question.
8H was glimpsed. From the mnemonic: <u>Ja</u>ckass <u>a</u>te <u>l</u>ive <u>t</u>ree, <u>k</u>ing intends to <u>f</u>ix several for <u>benign</u> <u>queen</u> – The underlined words are the values of the 5 cards before the 8H. So, the values of the cards removed were 4, 9, Q, J, A. The card glimpsed was a heart, so the suits can be determined. The five cards removed were: 4C, 9H, QS, JD, AS.

Since an 80% success rate is required, the magician should name 4 from this set and one other card not in this set. Answer (D).

31.

STEP 1 = > What do you need to determine to solve the problem?
How does a faro shuffle rearrange a JackAss deck?

STEP 2 = > What relevant data provided in this problem are necessary to answer the question?
The cyclical nature of a JackAss stack and the way a faro shuffle mixes the cards.

STEP 3 = > Use the relevant data to solve the question.
If a JackAss deck is split in two (for a faro shuffle), each half will have the same value of cards with the same colors at the same position in each half. If the top card of one half is 6C, 7H, 4S... then the top cards of the other half will be 6S, 7D, 4C. Interleaving these two groups will place the cards in pairs, by color. Suit order will change and the C, H, S, D pattern will disappear.

The cards will remain in JackAss order, except they will double up. Since 3 (tree) comes right after 5(live), answer (B).

32.

STEP 1 = > What do you need to determine to solve the problem?
How to apply the reordering from a faro shuffle to the given listing of a Stay-stack deck.

STEP 2 = > What relevant data provided in this problem are necessary to answer the question?
The center portion of an example Stay-stack and the earlier description of a faro shuffle.

STEP 3 = > Use the relevant data to solve the question.
In a faro shuffle, the deck is separated into two halves at the center. In this problem that would be between the two black kings. One will end up on top of the deck after the shuffle and the other on the bottom. KC top and KS bottom. Under the top KC there will be an indifferent card (one not given) and the the JS in the third position. Answer (C).

33.

STEP 1 = > What do you need to determine to solve the problem?
A method to track where cards move in a series of faro shuffles.

STEP 2 = > What relevant data provided in this problem are necessary to answer the question?
We are told that a faro shuffle doesn't disturb the pairing relationship in a Stay-stack deck, so we only need to find the number of shuffles it takes to return either card to the center.

STEP 3 = > Use the relevant data to solve the question.
After the first shuffle, the 4S will be on top.
The second shuffle puts it second.
Third shuffle → fourth.
Fourth shuffle → eighth.
Fifth shuffle → sixteenth.

Now it's in the bottom half of the packet. After the cards are separated to begin the next shuffle, it will be third (16 -13 = 3) down in a packet of 13 and after the shuffle, it will be fifth.

Sixth shuffle → fifth

Seventh shuffle→ tenth

Eighth shuffle → 20th

Ninth shuffle → 13th

This puts it back as one of the center two cards. Since a faro shuffle doesn't change the mirror image quality of Stay-stack, the 14th card will be the other black 4. Answer (C).

Printed in Great Britain
by Amazon